D1225636

BARI TASTY PURÉED & SOFT FOODS!

40 simple recipes to stop feeling overwhelmed after Bariatric Surgery

Your Onederland

Bariatric Community, Education & Support

ALL COPYRIGHTS RESERVED 2022

TO NEW BEGINNINGS

Maybe you're preparing for Bariatric Surgery and want to have all the right resources to get a head start.

Maybe you *just* had Bariatric Surgery, feeling overwhelmed and looking for simple recipes to get through the first stages of your journey.

Introducing Bari Tasty Puréed & Soft Foods! - your companion for the puréed and soft foods phases after bariatric surgery.

Now, you have access to 40 easy-to-follow recipes that will help you feel more in control.

You got this!

Your Onederland

DISCLAIMER

This book is made for educational, entertaining and inspirational purposes only and is not intended as personal or medical advice.

By reading this document, the reader acknowledges that the information provided in this book is not intended as nutritional, clinical, medical, legal or financial advice. Always consult a licensed specialist before attempting any techniques presented in this book.

All effort has been made to provide correct, acccurate and up to date information. No warranties of any kind are declared or implied.

By reading this document, the reader agrees that under no circumstances the author is responsible for any direct or indirect losses, as a result of the use of information of this document, including but not limited to inaccuracies, omissions or errors of any kind.

CONTENTS

Introduction

Bariatric Surgery is the most effective medical treatment for severe obesity and its related diseases.

But that doesn't mean that navigating your bariatric journey will be easy.

It doesn't mean that it's smooth sailing all the time.

Especially in the early stages when everything is still brand new. You may feel overwhelmed because:

- you're still recovering and feel sore
- you have head hunger, but HAVE TO follow your post-op diet
- you simply miss the joy of eating (regular) foods

Although you can't control everything that happens in your journey - you can learn about new recipes and find inspiration along the way.

And that's exactly why we created Bari Tasty Puréed & Soft Foods: to help you stay motivated, while you're discovering a whole new way of eating (and living!).

Before you try anything new, always make sure that you're cleared by your surgeon to do so.

The recipes in Bari Tasty Puréed & Soft Foods! are suitable for the puréed and soft foods stage, *after* you've completed the clear and full liquid stages.

With that being said, let's start with explaining what the post-op diet looks like. Next, we'll walk you through the bariatric "do's and don'ts" followed by discussing a few bariatric kitchen essentials and portion sizes.

The Post-Op Diet

The first days after surgery can be quite overwhelming. Dealing with gas pain, struggling to get your liquids in and meeting your protein goals - it can be a lot to process.

Everyone experiences the newly post operative - or *post-op* - stage differently, because no journey is the same.

Maybe you have little to no complications. Or maybe there are unexpected issues that make your post-op recovery more challenging.

Either way, there's one commonality that every bariatric patient has to commit to. A non-negotiable that's not an option - but truly a requirement.

Yes. We're talking about the bariatric surgery post-op diet.

What does the post-op diet look like?

While the pre-op diet is meant to shrink your liver prior to surgery - the post-op diet is intended to help your digestive system and pouch heal after surgery.

Your small stomach (pouch) is swollen and it's not possible to eat solid foods straight away. It's important to protect the sutures where your stomach was either removed or bypassed.

Your post-op diet consists of 4 or 5 different stages to slowly introduce different foods and textures back to your diet.

The post-op diet starts with clear liquids and ends with solid foods. Solid foods and a regular bariatric friendly diet to set the foundation for a lifelong balanced lifestyle.

The bariatric post-op diet generally lasts around 6-8 weeks. However, this time frame differs from person to person - depending whether there are any complications to consider and individual needs.

Not every surgical center will have the exact same guidelines when it comes down to the details of the post-op diet. But generally, the post-op diet has the following stages:

Tabel 1. The Bariatric Surgery Post Operative Diet Stages

STAGE	EXAMPLES	DURATION
Clear Liquids	Water, clear broth, diluted fruit juices no added sugars	Day 1-2
Full Liquids	Skim milk, protein shakes, low-fat yoghurt, strained soups	Day 3 - 14
Puréed Foods	Blended: chicken, turkey, tuna, haddock, tilapia, soups. Eggs, cottage cheese, oatmeal	Day 15 - 29
Soft Foods	Lean and moist meats, beans, lentils, tofu, white soft fish, mashed potatoes	Week 4 -6
Solid Foods	Regular foods that you're able to tolerate well at this point	> Week 6

Clear liquids. Once you wake up after your surgery, the challenge to stay hydrated begins. General guidelines state that you should aim for 48-64 oz (1.5 - 2 l) daily - taking small sips all day long.

Liquids that are allowed in this stage are: water, clear broth (tip: chicken broth is a high-protein liquid), diluted fruit juice without added sugars and decaffeinated tea.

Any caffeinated beverages should be avoided until you're cleared by your surgeon, about 30 days after your surgery.

Your pouch may not respond well to extreme cold or hot drinks yet. Try to tune into the signs of your pouch at all times.

Full liquids. The next step in your post-op diet is the full liquids stage where drinks such as skim milk, protein shakes (low-sugar, low-fat), yogurt and strained soups are allowed. Besides hydration, your protein intake is very important too.

Protein is the key macronutrient after bariatric surgery and supports the healing process. Also, protein prevents the breakdown of your muscle mass.

You probably won't meet all of your hydration and protein goals right off the bat.

For some people it may be easier to meet those goals, while others may still struggle years later. Keep in mind that everyone is different.

When you're trying to meet your hydration goals, it can be helpful to start with a high-protein liquid (such as a protein shake), followed by water. High-protein liquids are typically part of your 48-64 oz daily hydration goal.

Puréed Foods. So what are puréed foods exactly? Puréed foods require no chewing and are smooth - similar to apple sauce consistency. Examples of puréed foods are: blended chicken and fish, blended beans, cottage cheese and oatmeal (no chunks).

Remember, the focus should still be on protein first. If you have room for puréed vegetables they come next. And last, (your allowed) complex carbs.

At this stage, all foods that may cause digestive issues, such as bread, pasta, rice, spicy foods, high-fibrous vegetables, raw vegetables, fried foods, high-sugar foods and vegetables that cause gas, still need to be avoided.

Examples of vegetables that are allowed in the early stages post-op are spinach, butternut squash, carrots, green beans. All cooked and blended until puréed consistency.

Soft foods. The main difference between puréed foods and soft foods is the texture. Where puréed foods require no chewing, soft foods require little chewing and have a soft texture.

Examples of soft foods are: beans, lentils, eggs, cottage cheese, lean moist meats, canned fruit in own juice (no added sugars).

Some surgical centers allow more fruits and a wider array of complex carbs during this stage. While other surgeons recommend waiting until 6+ weeks post-op. *Always follow your surgeon's guidelines.*

Solid foods. The solid foods stage is the beginning of your regular lifelong diet after bariatric surgery. There may be some foods that you still won't tolerate at this point - but maybe later down the line, can enjoy again.

3 Things to keep in mind

The post-op diet progression is a journey on its own. Your entire eating experience will be different. Here are 3 things to consider when you're newly post-op:

1 Your tastebuds may change

It may take you by surprise that you might not like all foods and flavors similar to before surgery. Tastebuds can change. Maybe you can't stand sweet flavors anymore. Or perhaps there's specific foods that don't quite taste the same (or even make you nauseous). This is normal.

Find out which flavors work well for you - and build your meals from here.

2   Food intolerances are common after Bariatric Surgery

Having your digestive system surgically altered, often, goes hand-in-hand with food intolerances. One of those can be lactose intolerance.

Lactose intolerance is more common after mixed procedures like the Gastric Bypass, but it can also happen after a Gastric Sleeve.

But also, some foods are going to be more difficult to digest. These foods are often too:

- dry - like dry meat
- sticky - like glutenous rice
- fibrous - like asparagus
- spicy - like hot sauce
- gassy - like cabbage

Again, try to work with the foods that you can tolerate instead of pondering what you're missing out of. And always talk to your dietitian for tailor made advice.

3   Appetite, mind hunger & fullness cues

You won't experience appetite, hunger and fullness as before your surgery. And that's actually one of the reasons why bariatric surgery can be so effective.

Removing or bypassing the upper part of your stomach, also removes the part of your stomach (called the fundus) where the hunger hormone *ghrelin* is produced. This leads to a decrease of appetite and an increase in satiety.

Bariatric fullness cues to pay attention to are: hiccuping, burping, having a runny nose, sneezing and the physical sensation of fullness.

But just because your *physical appetite* is decreased, doesn't mean that *mind hunger* can't exist.

Actually, mind hunger after bariatric surgery can be worse, as it won't be possible to eat the foods that you might be craving.

Therefore, we truly hope that the recipes in this book will help you enjoy the foods within the realm of your possibilities - to keep you full and satisfied.

In the next chapter we'll discuss some of the most important do's and don'ts after bariatric surgery.

Bariatric Do's and Don'ts

Bariatric Surgery is so much more than losing weight fast. It's about creating habits that last. And to create a mindset that will help you maintain a lifestyle that will serve all your health and wellness goals.

Below, you'll find a few reminders for your bariatric journey to never forget.

Bariatric Surgery Do's:

- Do eat your protein first.
- Do stay hydrated while taking smalls sips.
- Do allow your pouch to fully heal after surgery.
- Do add high protein food sources to your diet.
- Do find out which foods work well for you and which ones don't.
- Do chew well and eat slow.
- Do separate solid foods from liquids.
- Do take your daily vitamins.
- Do ask your bariatric team for guidance.
- Do find the right support that suits your needs.
- Do give yourself grace.
- Do stay consistent and never give up.

Bariatric Surgery Don'ts:

- Don't move to the next stage of your post-op diet without your surgeon's clearance.
- Don't step on the scale every day. Weight fluctuates and also, the 3-week weight stall (and other stalls) are common after bariatric surgery.
- Don't skip meals. You'll need to eat 5-8 times daily to meet your hydration and protein requirements.
- Don't compare your journey to someone else.
- Don't continue to only rely on protein shakes once you're able to tolerate more foods well.
- Don't drink caffeine and alcohol until you're cleared by your surgeon to do so.

And always remember, bariatric surgery is a marathon - not a sprint. It's called bariatric surgery and not bariatric perfection. It's okay to make mistakes. This journey is a huge learning curve - and a continuous recommitment to yourself.

Bariatric Kitchen Essentials

Now, let's get back to the recipes. In this book you'll find 20 puréed recipes and 20 soft foods recipes. The aim of these dishes is to help you find inspiration with different flavors and varieties. So that you can enjoy food as much as possible in, what may be, the most challenging time when it comes down to getting used to your new stomach.

Cooking after Bariatric Surgery doesn't have to be complicated. Bariatric Nutrition should be simple and most of all sustainable for the long run.

Having the right kitchen tools are a must to make your life easier. And these kitchen essentials may come in handy after bariatric surgery:

- Food processor or blender (most recipes in this book require a food processor or blender - one of those will work just fine)
- Measuring cups
- Food scale
- Small plate (6-8 inches or 18-20 centimeters)
- Small utensils

How do I know which portion size is right for me?

All recipes in this book have a serving size. Remember, that these are not personal suggestions as portions fluctuate greatly and are different from person to person.

If you find the portions to large or too little, always adjust them to your own needs.

These are the general portion sizes that you may expect post-op:

Puréed: 1/4 cup Soft Foods: 1/2 cup	Solid Foods (start): 3/4 cup Solid Foods (ongoing): 1+ cup

20
PURÉED
RECIPES

Rosemary Chicken Salad

 Yield: 8 servings

 Time: 10 minutes

 1/4 cup = 1 serving*

*always follow your surgeon's guidelines and tune into your own hunger and fullness cues.

About this recipe

Chicken is an excellent source of protein. It's versatile and can be easily used in puréed and soft foods recipes.

Ingredients

- 4 oz (110 g) grilled chicken breast
- 1/2 cup (120 g) low-fat Greek yogurt
- 1/8 teaspoon rosemary powder
- Salt and pepper to taste
- Bone broth to desired texture

Directions

1. In a food processor, add the chicken, yogurt, rosemary and salt. Blend until smooth.
2. Add the bone broth until you have the desired texture.

Nutrition Facts

Per Serving

30 calories
Protein 5.5 g
Carbs 0.8 g
Fiber 0 g
Fat 0.6 g

Recipe Notes

- Substitute the chicken for tuna in brine.
- Substitute Greek yogurt for soy yogurt or lactose-free yogurt if you're lactose intolerant.
- If you don't have a food processor, you can use a blender instead.

Smooth Surimi Cream

 Yield: 8 servings

 Time: 15 minutes

1/4 cup = 1 serving*

*always follow your
surgeon's guidelines
and tune into your own
hunger and fullness
cues.

About this recipe

Surimi is a paste made from (white) fish. It's a more affordable option to real crab meat. With around 4 grams of protein per ounce - surimi is a great option to add to your bariatric diet.

Ingredients

- 4 oz (110 g) surimi chunks
- 1/2 cup (120 g) low-fat sour cream
- Salt and pepper to taste
- Water to desired texture

Directions

1. In a food processor, add the surimi chunks, sour cream, salt and pepper. Blend until smooth.
2. Add water until you have the desired texture.

Nutrition Facts
Per Serving

37 calories
Protein 1.4 g
Carbs 2.6 g
Fiber 0.1 g
Fat 2.3 g

Recipe Notes

- Substitute sour cream for low-fat Greek yogurt if you want to increase the amount of protein in this recipe.
- Substitute sour cream for soy yogurt if you can't tolerate dairy.
- If you don't have a food processor, you can use a blender instead.

Ricotta & Spinach Purée

 Yield: 8 servings

 Time: 15 minutes

 1/4 cup = 1 serving*

*always follow your surgeon's guidelines and tune into your own hunger and fullness cues.

About this recipe

One of the greatest early post-op side effects is constipation. But, why is that? Mostly, because of a lack of fiber, hydration and physical activity. Cooked spinach is one of the few vegetables that may be tolerated in the puréed stage - and immediately adds more fiber to your diet. It's a win-win right?

Ingredients

- 4 cups (240 g) spinach leaves
- 1 cup (250 g) low-fat ricotta cheese
- Salt and pepper to taste
- Bone broth to desired texture

Directions

1. Remove the stems from the spinach leaves, if there are any.
2. In a steaming pan, add the spinach leaves. Steam until fully cooked.
3. In a food processor, add the cooked spinach and ricotta. Blend until smooth.
4. Add bone broth until desired texture.

Nutrition Facts
Per Serving

44 calories
Protein 2.6 g
Carbs 1.4 g
Fiber 0.2 g
Fat 3.1 g

Recipe Notes

- If you can tolerate more herbs or spices, add them to this dish for some extra flavor.
- If you don't have a food processor, you can use a blender instead.

Basic Chicken Broth

 Yield: 8 servings

 Time: 3 1/2 hours

 1/4 cup = 1 serving*

*always follow your surgeon's guidelines and tune into your own hunger and fullness cues.

About this recipe

One of the most underrated protein food sources out there: basic chicken broth. Chicken bones contain collagen. When cooked, the collagen turns into gelatin which provides amino acids (the building blocks of protein).

Ingredients

- 2 1/2 pound bony chicken pieces
- 2 celery ribs with leaves, coarsely chopped
- 2 large carrots, coarsely chopped
- 2 yellow onions, cut in quarters
- 2 bay leaves
- 1/2 teaspoon thyme
- 32 oz (950 ml) cold water
- Salt and pepper to taste

Directions

1. In a soup kettle, or large pot, add all ingredients. Slowly bring to a boil. Reduce heat to simmer uncovered, about 3 hours. Skimming the foam during the process.
2. Remove from heat and allow to cool off.
3. Remove the chicken, and any other large pieces of food from the broth.
4. Strain the broth. Allow all small pieces of food to be removed, until you have a semi-clear broth.

Nutrition Facts
Per Serving

33 calories
Protein 5.3 g
Carbs 2.7 g
Fiber 0 g
Fat 0 g

Recipe Notes

- Make separate portions from the remainder of the broth and freeze.
- Chicken broth comes in handy when you want to liquify your puréed foods. Or to sip on as a separate meal (especially when restriction feels high).

Black Bean Soup

 Yield: 8 servings

 Time: 40 minutes

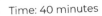 1/4 cup = 1 serving*

*always follow your
surgeon's guidelines
and tune into your own
hunger and fullness
cues.

About this recipe

Black beans, provide about 8 grams per 1/2 cup. So, it
goes without saying that beans are a great plant-based
protein source to add to your post-op diet.

Ingredients

- 1 tablespoon olive oil
- 7.5 oz (1/2 can, 210 g) black
  beans, rinsed and drained
- 16 oz (430 ml) chicken
  broth
- 1/8 teaspoon cumin
  powder
- 1/8 teaspoon turmeric
  powder
- 1 bay leaf
- Salt and pepper to taste

Toppings (optional)
- Mashed avocado

Directions

1. In a large pot, heat the olive oil over medium heat.
   Add the black beans, stirring occasionally, about 5
   minutes.
2. Add chicken broth and bring to a boil over
   medium-high heat. Lower heat to a simmer.
3. Stir in the cumin powder and turmeric powder. Add
   the bay leaf.
4. Allow to simmer, about 25 minutes.
5. Remove the bay leaf with a spoon and turn off the
   heat.
6. Allow to cool off before handling the soup.
7. In a food processor, add the soup. Blend until
   completely smooth. Add more broth if desired.

Nutrition Facts
Per Serving

62 calories
Protein 3.5 g
Carbs 6.3 g
Fiber 4.6 g
Fat 1.8 g

Recipe Notes

- Substitute chicken broth for vegetable broth if
  you're looking for a vegan variety. Keep in mind
  that chicken broth contains protein, vegetable
  broth doesn't.
- Did you know that legumes are relatively higher in
  complex carbs? But also offer protein and other
  valuable nutrients like iron.
- If you don't have a food processor, you can use a
  blender instead.

*whole beans, avocado and parsley for garnish - not for consumption at this stage

21

Peach & Yogurt Parfait

 Yield: 6 servings

 Time: 10 minutes

 1/4 cup = 1 serving*

*always follow your surgeon's guidelines and tune into your own hunger and fullness cues.

About this recipe

Fresh fruit should be avoided until you're cleared by your surgeon. And typically, you'll start with canned fruit instead. Make sure to use canned fruit in water or its own juice (not in syrup) as the extra sugars may cause digestive issues.

Ingredients

- 8.5 oz (1 small can, 230 g) peaches in own juice
- 1 cup (240 g) low-fat Greek yogurt
- 1/8 teaspoon cinnamon powder

Directions

1. In a food processor, add the peaches. Blend until smooth.
2. In a small glass, spoon in 1/2 of Greek yogurt. Top with 1/2 of peach purée.
3. In another glass, repeat step 2.

Nutrition Facts
Per Serving

38 calories
Protein 3.7 g
Carbs 5 g
Fiber 0.5 g
Fat 0 g

Recipe Notes

- Store the other serving in the fridge up to 24 hours.
- Substitute Greek yogurt for soy yogurt or lactose-free yogurt if you're lactose intolerant.
- Adjust the amount of peaches accordingly. If you're restriction is very high, omit some of the peach puree so you'll have more space for your yogurt.
- If you don't have a food processor, you can use a blender instead.

Creamy Cod Purée

Yield: 4 servings

Time: 30 minutes

1/4 cup = 1 serving*

*always follow your surgeon's guidelines and tune into your own hunger and fullness cues.

About this recipe

Cod is a great addition to the puréed stage, because it's soft (which makes it easy to blend). But it's not just the texture that makes cod a winner, it's also the high amount of protein that helps you meet your protein goals right after surgery.

Ingredients

- 8 ounces (220 g) cod
- 1 teaspoon Italian seasoning
- 1 tablespoon olive oil
- 4 tablespoons low-fat mayonnaise
- Salt and pepper to taste
- Water to desired texture

Directions

1. In a bowl, add the cod and the herbs. Mix until fully coated.
2. In a pan, add olive oil and heat over medium heat. And add the cod. Bake, about 10 minutes, turning the cod halfway.
3. Remove the cod from pan.
4. In a food processor, add the cod and mayonnaise. Blend until smooth.
5. Add salt and pepper to taste.
6. Add water until you have the desired texture.

Nutrition Facts
Per Serving

125 calories
Protein 12 g
Carbs 1.7 g
Fiber 0 g
Fat 7.8 g

Recipe Notes

- If you don't have Italian herbs in your pantry, try a combination of the following (if tolerated well): oregano powder, marjoram leaf powder, coriander powder, basil powder, rosemary powder.
- Substitute the cod for any other white, soft fish.
- If you don't have a food processor, you can use a blender instead.

Smoked Salmon Mousse

 Yield: 8 servings

 Time: 10 minutes

 1/4 cup = 1 serving*

*always follow your surgeon's guidelines and tune into your own hunger and fullness cues.

About this recipe

Besides protein, salmon is a great source of healthy fats too. Because of its nutrient density, you may find yourself quite full after eating this salmon mousse.

Ingredients

- 8 ounces (220 g) smoked salmon
- 1 cup (225 g) cottage cheese
- 1 teaspoon dill powder
- Salt and pepper to taste

Directions

1. In a food processor, add the salmon, cottage cheese and dill powder. Blend until smooth.
2. Add salt and pepper to taste.

Nutrition Facts
Per Serving

78 calories
Protein 9.2 g
Carbs 0.9 g
Fiber 0 g
Fat 4.1 g

Recipe Notes

- If you're cleared by your surgeon to have a splash of lemon juice - add lemon juice to the mixture before blending it to give this recipe some 'zest'.
- Substitute the cottage cheese for Greek yogurt if you don't like cottage cheese.
- Fresh herbs are typically still avoided at this stage.
- If you don't have a food processor, you can use a blender instead.

*fresh dill for garnish - not for consumption at this stage

Refried Bean Purée

 Yield: 12 servings

 Time: 20 minutes

1/4 cup = 1 serving*

*always follow your surgeon's guidelines and tune into your own hunger and fullness cues.

About this recipe

With more than 5 grams of fiber per serving, you can be sure that this recipe will help you boost your fiber needs. But it's not just the fiber that make this a great recipe in the puréed stage. Beans will help you meet your protein goals better too!

Ingredients

- 15 oz (1 can, 425 g) pinto beans, rinsed and drained
- 1 tablespoon olive oil
- 8 oz (230 ml) chicken broth
- 1/8 teaspoon cumin powder
- 1/8 teaspoon onion powder
- 1/8 teaspoon garlic powder
- Salt and pepper to taste

Toppings (optional)
- Low-fat sour cream
- Low-fat Greek yogurt

Directions

1. In a sauce pan, add 1 tablespoon of olive oil and heat over medium heat.
2. Add the rinsed and drained pinto beans and fry for 1 minute while stirring.
3. Lower heat and add the chicken broth. Bring slowly to a boil while adding the cumin powder, onion powder, garlic powder, salt and pepper. Boil, about 10 minutes.
4. In a food processor, add the beans. Blend until smooth.
5. Top with low-fat sour cream or Greek yogurt if desired.

Recipe Notes

- Substitute the chicken broth for vegetable broth (keep in mind that chicken broth has more protein than vegetable broth).
- Omit the herbs if you can't tolerate them well. Adjust the amount of herbs to your own needs.
- Make sure to rinse the beans well before using them.
- If you don't have a food processor, you can use a blender instead.

Nutrition Facts
Per Serving

46 calories
Protein 2.3 g
Carbs 5.7 g
Fiber 1.3 g
Fat 1.2 g

*fresh parsley and grated cheddar for garnish, not for consumption at this stage.

Easy Egg Salad

 Yield: 2 servings

 Time: 10 minutes

 1/4 cup = 1 serving*

*always follow your surgeon's guidelines and tune into your own hunger and fullness cues.

About this recipe

Eggs provide about 6 grams of protein per egg. They can be scrambled, boiled - and then blended in the puréed stage. Besides protein, eggs (yolks) are a great source of choline, which supports a healthy nervous system.

Ingredients

- 1 hard boiled egg
- 2 tablespoons low-fat Greek yogurt
- 1/8 teaspoon parsley powder
- Salt and pepper to taste

Directions

1. In a food processor, add the egg, Greek yogurt and parsley powder. Blend until smooth.
2. Add salt and pepper to taste.

Nutrition Facts
Per Serving

44 calories
Protein 4.8 g
Carbs 1 g
Fiber 0 g
Fat 2.2 g

Recipe Notes

- Substitute Greek yogurt for low-fat mayonnaise for a different flavor. Keep in mind that mayonnaise has less protein and more (satuated) fat than Greek yogurt.
- If you don't have a food processor, you can use a blender instead.
- Use dried parsley instead if you don't have parsley powder. Only when cleared by your surgeon.

*fresh parsley and egg toppings for garnish, not for consumption at this stage.

Coconut Lentil Soup

 Yield: 16 servings

 Time: 20 minutes

 1/4 cup = 1 serving*

*always follow your surgeon's guidelines and tune into your own hunger and fullness cues.

About this recipe

Soups are one of the most versatile puréed dishes in this stage. Enjoy this creamy lentil soup with a surprising coconut twist.

Ingredients

- 15 oz (1 can, 425 g) lentils, rinsed and drained
- 8 oz (230 ml) vegetable broth
- 1 cup (230 ml) low-fat coconut milk
- 1/8 teaspoon cumin powder
- 1/8 teaspoon onion powder
- 1/8 teaspoon garlic powder
- Salt and pepper to taste

Directions

1. In a soup kettle add lentils and vegetable broth. Slowly bring to a boil.
2. Stir in coconut milk, cumin powder, onion powder, garlic powder, salt and pepper. Stir until well combined. Boil, about 5 minutes.
3. Allow the lentil soup to cool off before handling.
4. Add lentil soup to a blender. Blend until smooth.

Nutrition Facts
Per Serving

52 calories
Protein 2.4 g
Carbs 3.8 g
Fiber 1 g
Fat 2.8 g

Recipe Notes

- Add low-fat sour cream as a topping if tolerated well.
- Substitute the lentils for any other type of canned legumes.
- You can use dried lentils (or legumes) too. Make sure to cook them thoroughly until softened.

Sweet Potato Queso

Yield: 8 servings

Time: 25 minutes

1/4 cup = 1 serving*

*always follow your surgeon's guidelines and tune into your own hunger and fullness cues.

About this recipe

But aren't sweet potatoes loaded with sugar? No, they most certainly are not. Although they're a tad bit higher in carbs than regular potatoes - those are mainly complex carbs providing you with much needed fiber as well.

Ingredients

- 1 small sweet potato, peeled and chopped
- 8 oz (230 ml) water
- 1 bay leaf
- 1/2 cup (120 g) low-fat Greek yogurt
- 1/8 teaspoon onion powder
- 1/8 teaspoon garlic powder
- 1/8 teaspoon paprika powder
- 1 tablespoon nutritional yeast
- Salt and pepper to taste

Directions

1. In a sauce pan, add the chopped sweet potato, water and bay leaf. Bring to a boil on medium-high heat. Boil, about 15 minutes until sweet potatoes are soft.
2. Allow the sweet potatoes to cool off. Remove the bay leaf.
3. In a food processor, add the sweet potatoes, Greek yogurt, onion powder, garlic powder, paprika powder, nutritional yeast, salt and pepper. Blend until smooth. Add more Greek yogurt if needed.

Nutrition Facts
Per Serving

38 calories
Protein 3.5 g
Carbs 5.6 g
Fiber 0.3 g
Fat 0.1 g

Recipe Notes

- Did you know that 1 tablespoon of nutritional yeast contains 4 grams of protein?
- Nutritional yeast has a 'cheesy' flavor and is often used as a substitute for cheese in vegan dishes.
- Also, nutritional yeast is a *complete protein* meaning that it provides ALL 9 essential amino acids, like animal protein does.
- If you don't have a food processor, you can use a blender instead.

*fresh thyme for garnish, not for consumption at this stage.

Chicken Chili

 Yield: 12 servings

 Time: 45 minutes

 1/4 cup = 1 serving*

*always follow your surgeon's guidelines and tune into your own hunger and fullness cues.

About this recipe

Red meat, like lamb and beef are often not tolerated great at this stage of your journey. By substituting the beef for chicken, you can still enjoy this nice dish.

Ingredients

- 4 oz (110 g) chicken breast
- 8 oz (230 ml) chicken broth
- 1 bay leaf
- 1 tablespoon olive oil
- 1 cup (230 ml) marinara sauce
- 1/2 cup (100 g) canned kidney beans, rinsed and drained
- 1 teaspoon cilantro powder
- Salt and pepper to taste

Toppings (optional)
- Low-fat sour cream
- Low-fat Greek yogurt

Nutrition Facts
Per Serving

39 calories
Protein 3.2 g
Carbs 3.3 g
Fiber 0.8 g
Fat 1.3 g

Directions

1. In a pot, add chicken breast, chicken broth and bay leaf. Slowly bring to a boil over medium heat. Lower heat and boil, about 20 minutes.
2. Remove chicken breast from pot and allow to cool off.
3. Shred the chicken, once cooled off enough to handle.
4. In a pan over medium-high heat, heat olive oil. Add the shredded chicken, marinara sauce, kidney beans, salt, pepper and cilantro powder. Slowly bring to a simmer. Simmer, about 15 minutes.
5. Remove from heat and allow to cool off before handling.
6. In a food processor, add the chicken-marinara mixture and blend until smooth.
7. Serve with low-fat sour cream or low-fat Greek yogurt.

Recipe Notes

- Substitute the chicken breast for ground turkey. Skip step 1-3, but make sure to thoroughly cook the ground turkey before adding the marina sauce and kidney beans.

Butternut Squash Soup

Yield: 12 servings

Time: 40 minutes

Add flavorless protein powder

1/4 cup = 1 serving*

*always follow your surgeon's guidelines and tune into your own hunger and fullness cues.

About this recipe

Butternut squash is one of the few vegetables that's typically allowed in the puréed stage. Once cooked, it's soft texture allows you to create a great puréed recipe instantly. Like this butternut squash soup!

Ingredients

- 1 small butternut squash, peeled and chopped
- 16 oz (430 ml) chicken broth
- 1/2 teaspoon rosemary powder
- 1/2 teaspoon oregano powder
- 2 scoops unflavored protein powder
- Salt and pepper to taste

Directions

1. In a large pot over medium-high heat, add the butternut squash, chicken broth, rosemary powder, oregano powder, salt and pepper. Slowly bring to a boil. Lower heat and simmer, about 30 minutes.
2. Stir in the protein powder until blended well.
3. In a blender, add the soup. Blend until smooth.

Nutrition Facts
Per Serving

50 calories
Protein 4 .7 g
Carbs 2.9 g
Fiber 0.5 g
Fat 2.1 g

Recipe Notes

- You could use vegetable broth instead of chicken broth. Keep in mind that chicken broth has protein and vegetable broth doesn't.
- Substitute the rosemary powder and oregano powder for curry powder if you can tolerate those spices already *and more importantly* when cleared by your surgeon.
- Roast the pumpkin before adding it to the pot to create a rich flavor.

Pear & Cottage Cheese

 Yield: 2 servings

 Time: 5 minutes

1/4 cup = 1 serving*

*always follow your surgeon's guidelines and tune into your own hunger and fullness cues.

About this recipe

Cottage cheese. You either love it or hate it. Or you've learned to tolerate it once you've entered the puréed stage. Cottage cheese is one of the most underrated high-protein foods with about 25 grams of protein per cup.

Ingredients

- 1 small pear, peeled and chopped
- 1/8 teaspoon cinnamon powder
- 1 teaspoon unsweetened apple sauce
- 1/2 cup (110 g) cottage cheese

Topping (optional)
- Zero-sugar vanilla extract

Directions

1. In a bowl, add the chopped pear and cinnamon. Microwave, about 30 seconds.
2. Add the unsweetened apple sauce and mash the pear until puréed texture.
3. In a food processor, add the cottage cheese. Mix until smooth.
4. In a small glass, add one layer of cottage cheese. Next, one layer of the puréed pear.
5. Drizzle with zero-sugar vanilla extract if desired.

Nutrition Facts
Per Serving

68 calories
Protein 6.2 g
Carbs 5 g
Fiber 0.6 g
Fat 2.2 g

Recipe Notes

- If you can't stomach cottage cheese, use 1/2 cup of low-fat Greek yogurt instead.
- If you're looking for a vegan alternative, substitute the cottage cheese for soy yogurt.
- Add skim milk to the mixture to liquify the texture if needed.
- Instead of mashing the pear with a fork, you could use a food processor as well.
- Add more unsweetened apple sauce if you want to adjust the texture even more.

Smooth Tuna Salad

 Yield: 4 servings

 Time: 10 minutes

 1/4 cup = 1 serving*

*always follow your surgeon's guidelines and tune into your own hunger and fullness cues.

About this recipe

Canned tuna is a great food source when choosing your protein in the soft foods stage. Did you know that tuna has about 8 grams of protein per ounce?

Ingredients

- 5 oz tuna (1 can, 140 g), in brine, not drained
- 2 tablespoons low-fat mayonnaise
- Salt and pepper to taste
- Water to desired texture

Directions

1. In a food processor, add the tuna including the water, mayonnaise, salt and pepper. Blend until smooth.
2. Add more water until you have the desired texture

Nutrition Facts
Per Serving

78 calories
Protein 8.8 g
Carbs 0.9 g
Fiber 0 g
Fat 4.3 g

Recipe Notes

- Substitute the low-fat mayonnaise for low-fat (Greek) yogurt to increase the protein of this recipe.

Tasty Tzatziki

 Yield: 4 servings

 Time: 10 minutes

1/4 cup = 1 serving*

*always follow your
surgeon's guidelines
and tune into your own
hunger and fullness
cues.

About this recipe

If you're tired of eating plain Greek yogurt and are
looking for something refreshing - then this Tasty
Tzatziki is definitely worth trying. Omit the lemon juice
if you're not cleared to have citrus juices yet. And come
back to this recipe adding that zest later when you're a
bit further out!

Ingredients

- 1 cup (240 g) low-fat Greek
  yogurt
- 1/2 teaspoon garlic powder
- 1 teaspoon dill powder
- Salt and pepper to taste

Optional
- Lemon juice*
- Lemon zest*

Directions

1. In a mixing bowl, add the Greek yogurt, garlic
   powder, dill powder, salt and pepper.
2. Mix until well combined.

Nutrition Facts
Per Serving

33 calories
Protein 4.9 g
Carbs 3 g
Fiber 0 g
Fat 0.1 g

Recipe Notes

- Use fresh minced garlic instead of the garlic
  powder if tolerated well and approved by your
  surgeon.
- Use fresh finely chopped dill instead of dill powder
  if tolerated well and approved by your surgeon.
- *Only add citrus juice when approved by your
  surgeon. Citrus may irritate the pouch.

Pineapple (N)ice Cream

Yield: 6 servings

Prep time: 10 minutes
Freeze time: 8 hours

1/4 cup = 1 serving*

*always follow your
surgeon's guidelines
and tune into your own
hunger and fullness
cues.

About this recipe

Make sure to use canned pineapple in water or 100%
juice (not syrup) to avoid any added sugars that may
cause digestive issues at this stage. Tip: add unflavored
protein powder to this recipe to increase the amount
of protein.

Ingredients

- 8 oz (1 can, 200 g)
  pineapple chunks, in
  water or 100% juice,
  drained
- 1 cup (240 ml) buttermilk

You'll also need:
- Popsicle molds
- Popsicle sticks (if the
  molds don't include the
  sticks already)

Directions

1. In a food processor, add the pineapple chunks and
   butter milk. Blend until smooth.
2. Pour the pineapple mixture in the popsicle molds.
3. Place in freezer and allow to fully set for at least 8
   hours.

Nutrition Facts
Per Serving

24 calories
Protein 1 g
Carbs 4.6 g
Fiber 0.2 g
Fat 0.1 g

Recipe Notes

- If you're using separate (wooden) popsicle sticks -
  place the molds in the freezer without the sticks
  for 2 hours. Next, add the popsicle sticks so they
  stay in place.
- Substitute the pineapple for (canned) peaches or
  any other peeled and soft fruit that you're cleared
  to eat in this stage.
- If you don't have a food processor, you can use a
  blender instead.

Cinnamon Apple Sauce

Yield: 2 servings

Time: 10 minutes

Add flavorless protein powder

1/4 cup = 1 serving*

*always follow your
surgeon's guidelines
and tune into your own
hunger and fullness
cues.

About this recipe

If you're craving something sweet, then this recipe
might be just what you need. It's simple. It's sweet
from the natural sugars (fructose) from the apples. And
that extra touch of cinnamon makes this homemade
apple sauce a real delight!

Ingredients

- 1 apple, peeled and finely
  chopped
- 1/2 teaspoon cinnamon
  powder
- 1 scoop unflavored protein
  powder
- Water to taste

Directions

1. In a bowl, add the chopped apple. Microwave,
   about 2 minutes.
2. In a food processor, add the warmed apple,
   cinnamon powder and protein powder. Blend until
   smooth
3. Add water to adjust the texture of the apple sauce,
   if desired.

Nutrition Facts
Per Serving

116 calories
Protein 12.6 g
Carbs 9.4 g
Fiber 1 g
Fat 3.1 g

Recipe Notes

- You could use vanilla flavored protein powder too,
  if you want to create a different flavor.
- Did you know that whey protein is absorbed
  quicker than casein protein? Make sure to discuss
  your options with your dietitian first.
- If you don't have a food processor, you can use a
  blender instead.

Low-Fat Vanilla Custard

 Yield: 4 servings

 Time: 15 minutes

 1/4 cup = 1 serving*

*always follow your surgeon's guidelines and tune into your own hunger and fullness cues.

About this recipe

If you're craving something sweet, then this low-fat baked custard may be just what you need.

Ingredients

- 8 oz (230 ml) skim milk
- 3 tablespoons granulated sweetener
- 1 teaspoon corn flour
- 2 medium egg yolks
- 1/2 teaspoon vanilla extract

Topping (optional)
- Cinnamon powder

Directions

1. In a sauce pan over low heat, slowly bring the skim milk to a simmer. Remove from heat.
2. In a mixing bowl, add the sweetener, corn flour, egg yolks and vanilla extract. Whisk until well combined.
3. Slowly and gradually, whisk in the warm milk.
4. Using a strain, slowly whisk the milk mixture into the pan over low heat. Stir until the custard thickens and has the desired texture.

Nutrition Facts
Per Serving

87 calories
Protein 4.7 g
Carbs 6 g
Fiber 0 g
Fat 4.9 g

Recipe Notes

- Avoid any added sugars at this stage.
- Substitute the skimmed milk for soy milk or lactose-free milk if you're lactose intolerant
- Add a scoop of vanilla powder to increase the amount of protein in this recipe and to intensify the flavor.

20
SOFT FOODS
RECIPES

Lime & Pepper Tilapia

 Yield: 2 servings

 Time: 30 minutes

 1/2 cup = 1 serving*

*always follow your surgeon's guidelines and tune into your own hunger and fullness cues.

About this recipe

White fish, like tilapia is a great way to get your protein in during the soft foods stage. Its soft, flaky texture usually sits well in a small bariatric pouch.

Ingredients

- 1 tilapia fillet (4 oz, 110 g)
- 1 tablespoon olive oil
- 1 tablespoon lime juice*
- 1/4 teaspoon ground black pepper
- 1/4 teaspoon dill powder
- Salt to taste

Directions

1. Preheat oven to 400°F (200°C).
2. In a small bowl, add the olive oil, lime juice, black pepper and dill powder. Mix until well combined.
3. In a baking pan, add the fillet and coat the tilapia fillet with the olive oil mixture.
4. Place in oven until fully cooked, about 20 minutes.

Nutrition Facts
Per Serving

95 calories
Protein 9.9 g
Carbs 0.4 g
Fiber 0 g
Fat 5.9 g

Recipe Notes

- Omit or dilute the lime juice with water, if you can't tolerate this well (yet).
- Substitute the tilapia fillet for any other white (soft) fish.
- *Only add lime juice when cleared by your surgeon. Citrus fruit may irritate the pouch.

Egg & Avocado Mash

 Yield: 2 servings

 Time: 10 minutes

1/2 cup = 1 serving*

*always follow your
surgeon's guidelines
and tune into your own
hunger and fullness
cues.

About this recipe

If you're craving food with a little bit of substance, this recipe is for you. Both eggs and avocado are quite filling due to the protein in eggs and the unsaturated fats in avocado.

Ingredients

- 1 avocado, peeled and pitted
- 2 hard boiled eggs
- Salt and pepper to taste

Directions

1. In a bowl, add the avocado and eggs. Mash with a fork until desired texture.
2. Add salt and pepper to taste.
3. Serve immediately.

Nutrition Facts
Per Serving

233 calories
Protein 8 g
Carbs 1.6 g
Fiber 2.8 g
Fat 21 g

Recipe Notes

- Sprinkle a little bit of lemon juice on the mash to prevent the avocado turning brown.
- Reduce the amount of avocado per serving if it's too filling due to the unsaturated fats.
- Serve this dish immediately as avocado tends to turn brown quick.

Single Serving Ricotta Bake

 Yield: 1 serving

 Time: 30 minutes

 1/2 cup = 1 serving*

*always follow your surgeon's guidelines and tune into your own hunger and fullness cues.

About this recipe

This warm single serving ricotta bake is a perfect dish when you're looking for something savory and want to meet your protein goals better. The soft texture of ricotta integrates well with the requirements of this stage of your journey (and later on too!).

Ingredients

- 1/2 cup (75 g) low-fat ricotta cheese
- 1 egg, lightly beaten
- 1/8 teaspoon Italian seasoning
- 1 tablespoon marinara sauce

Directions

1. Preheat oven to 350°F (175°C).
2. In a mixing bowl, add the ricotta, egg and Italian seasoning. Whisk until well combined.
3. In a oven-safe single serve baking dish, add the ricotta mixture.
4. Top with the marinara sauce.
5. Place in oven until cooked, about 20 minutes.

Nutrition Facts
Per Serving

206 calories
Protein 14.2 g
Carbs 4 g
Fiber 0 g
Fat 14.8 g

Recipe Notes

- Omit the marina sauce if you just want the ricotta bake.
- Add layers of grilled zucchini or eggplant when moving on to the solids stage for a different variety of traditional lasagna.

*mint for garnish, not for consumption at this stage.

BBQ Chicken Salad

 Yield: 3 servings

 Time: 10 minutes

 1/2 cup = 1 serving*

*always follow your surgeon's guidelines and tune into your own hunger and fullness cues.

About this recipe

Have you been craving BBQ chicken but you're not sure how to incorporate this in the soft foods stage? Well, with this 2-step zero-sugar BBQ chicken salad, it's a win-win. Both the flavor and the amount of protein will be just what you need.

Ingredients

- 4 oz (110 g) grilled chicken breast
- 1/2 cup (120 g) low-fat Greek yogurt
- 1 tablespoon zero-sugar BBQ sauce
- Salt and pepper to taste

Directions

1. In a food processor, add the chicken, Greek yogurt and zero-sugar BBQ sauce. Blend until smooth.
2. Add salt and pepper to taste.

Nutrition Facts
Per Serving

91 calories
Protein 13.7 g
Carbs 2.2 g
Fiber 2.9 g
Fat 0.1 g

Recipe Notes

- To keep it simple, use ready-to-use rotisserie chicken.
- Zero-sugar products are often sweetened with sugar alcohols (like erythritol). Be mindful about those sugar alcohols as they can cause irritability and digestive issues.
- If you don't have a food processor, you can use a blender instead.

Curry Deviled Eggs

 Yield: 4 servings

 Time: 10 minutes

 1/2 cup = 1 serving*

*always follow your surgeon's guidelines and tune into your own hunger and fullness cues.

About this recipe

Not only are deviled eggs a delicious snack to meet your protein goals, they also make great party snack that the whole family can enjoy.

Ingredients

- 4 hard boiled eggs
- 1/4 cup (60 g) low-fat Greek yogurt
- 1/4 teaspoon curry powder
- Salt to taste

Directions

1. Peel the eggs and carefully cut them lengthways i half. Remove the yolk from the eggs.
2. In a bowl, add the egg yolks, Greek yogurt and curry powder. Mash until softened. Add salt to tast
3. Scoop the curry-yolk mixture into the egg white halves.
4. Serve immediately.

Nutrition Facts
Per Serving

72 calories
Protein 7.4 g
Carbs 0.8 g
Fiber 0 g
Fat 4.4 g

Recipe Notes

- Use a piping bag if you want to present the deviled eggs more neatly.
- If you don't have curry powder - try these herbs instead (if cleared by your surgeon and tolerated well): turmeric powder, garlic powder, onion powder, cilantro powder, ground black pepper and salt.
- Substitute the Greek yogurt for soy yogurt or lactose-free yogurt if you're lactose intolerant.

*parsley for garnish, not for consumption at this stage.

Turkey Marinara Meat Balls

Yield: 8 servings

Time: 30 minutes

1/2 cup = 1 serving*

*always follow your
surgeon's guidelines
and tune into your own
hunger and fullness
cues.

About this recipe

Did you know that ground turkey is often better
tolerated at this stage than ground beef? These turkey
marinara meat balls make an excellent warm meal.
Serve with mashed (sweet) potatoes, if you've got any
space left in your new stomach.

Ingredients

- 1 lb (450 g) lean ground
  turkey
- 1 egg
- 1/2 teaspoon paprika
  powder
- 1/4 teaspoon cumin
  powder
- 1/4 teaspoon onion
  powder
- 1/4 teaspoon garlic powder
- 1 tablespoon olive oil
- 16 oz (500 ml) marinara
  sauce

Toppings (optional)
- Chopped basil leaves
- Chopped parsley

Nutrition Facts
Per Serving

140 calories
Protein 13.8 g
Carbs 4.3 g
Fiber 1.1 g
Fat 7.2 g

Directions

1. In a mixing bowl, add the turkey, egg, paprika
   powder, cumin powder, onion powder, garlic
   powder, salt and pepper. Knead the turkey with
   your hands until all ingredients are well combined.
2. Using your hands, knead the turkey in small balls,
   about 2 inches in diameter.
3. In a pan, heat olive oil over medium-high heat. Add
   the turkey balls. Turn regularly and brown all
   around.
4. Lower heat, and add the marinara sauce. Close the
   lid and continue to simmer until fully cooked, about
   20 minutes.

Recipe Notes

- Only add the basil leaves and fresh parsley when
  cleared by your surgeon and if tolerated well.
- If the turkey mixture is too sticky to handle, add 1
  tablespoon of all-purpose flour.
- You can also make the marinara sauce yourself by
  blending (peeled) fresh tomatoes or canned
  tomatoes in a blender or food processor.
- If you can tolerated onion and garlic well, you can
  omit the onion and garlic powder and use sautéed
  onions and garlic instead.

65

Simple Scrambled Eggs

Yield: 2 servings

Time: 10 minutes

1/2 cup = 1 serving*

*always follow your surgeon's guidelines and tune into your own hunger and fullness cues.

About this recipe

One of the most convenient post-op foods: eggs. They're nutritious, they're soft and they're packed with important nutrients, like choline and of course - protein!

Ingredients

- 1 tablespoon olive oil
- 2 eggs
- 1/4 cup (60 ml) skim milk
- Salt and pepper to taste

Directions

1. In a mixing bowl, crack the eggs and add the skim milk. Whisk for about 30-60 seconds. Add salt and pepper.
2. In a skillet, heat the olive oil over medium heat.
3. Lower the heat, and pour the egg mixture into the skillet.
4. With a spatula, scramble the eggs from the sides to the centre. Keep scrambling the eggs to make sure they don't stick to the surface of the skillet. Keep the heat low.
5. Remove the scrambled eggs from the heat when cooked and serve immediately.

Nutrition Facts
Per Serving

121 calories
Protein 7.3 g
Carbs 1.6 g
Fiber 0 g
Fat 9.5 g

Recipe Notes

- Scrambled eggs can turn from fluffy to burnt real fast if you don't continue to use the spatula to scrape the edges of the egg to the center of the skillet.
- You could also add grated cheese to the mixture, when approved by your surgeon and if tolerated well.

Pronto Pesto Chicken

 Yield: 2 servings

 Time: 30 minutes

1/2 cup = 1 serving*

*always follow your surgeon's guidelines and tune into your own hunger and fullness cues.

About this recipe

Pronto means "fast" in Italian. And besides delicious, this Pronto Pesto Chicken is a quick meal indeed.

Ingredients

- 1 chicken breast fillet (6 ounces, 170 g)
- 1 tablespoon olive oil
- 1 cup (230 ml) bone broth

For the Bariatric Friendly Pesto:
- 20 basil leaves, blanched
- 2 tablespoons pine nuts
- 2 tablespoons grated Parmesan cheese
- 1 tablespoon olive oil
- Salt and pepper to taste

Directions

To make the pesto:
1. In a food processor, add the blanched basil leaves, pine nuts, cheese, olive oil, salt and pepper. Blend until smooth.

Continue cooking:
1. In a ziplock bag, add the chicken breast fillet and the pesto. Close the bag and rub the pesto on the chicken breast until fully coated.
2. In a skillet, heat olive oil over medium-high heat. Add the chicken breast. Cook, about 5 minutes on each side.
3. Add the bone broth and cover the lid. Cook, until chicken is done, about 15-20 minutes.

Nutrition Facts
Per Serving

186 calories
Protein 22 g
Carbs 1.5 g
Fiber 0.3 g
Fat 10.2 g

Recipe Notes

- Make sure that you're cleared by your surgeon to include home made pesto in your post-op diet.
- Chicken breast tends to get "dry" easily. Add as much bone broth as needed for extra moisture.
- If you don't have a food processor, you can use a blender instead.

69

Taco Tofu Bites

 Yield: 4 servings

 Time: 20 minutes

 1/2 cup = 1 serving*

*always follow your surgeon's guidelines and tune into your own hunger and fullness cues.

About this recipe

Tofu is probably one of the best plant-based high protein food sources to use as a substitute for poultry, meat or seafood. Did you know that tofu has about 8 grams of protein per 3-ounce serving?

Ingredients

- 14 oz (400 g) extra firm tofu
- 1 teaspoon taco seasoning
- 1 tablespoon olive oil

Directions

1. Using a clean kitchen towel, squeeze all the extra moisture from the tofu.
2. Cut the tofu into small equal sized squares.
3. In a mixing bowl add the tofu and taco seasoning. Mix until fully coated.
4. In a skillet, heat olive oil over medium-high heat. Add the tofu squares. Flip regularly until golden brown, about 15 minutes.
5. Serve immediately.

Nutrition Facts
Per Serving

136 calories
Protein 11.6 g
Carbs 9.4 g
Fiber 0.3 g
Fat 9.4 g

Recipe Notes

- If you don't have taco seasoning try this combination of herbs instead: paprika powder, oregano powder, garlic powder, onion powder and salt.
- Crushed chili flakes are often used in taco seasoning, but you may want to omit too much spices as they can irritate your pouch.

Egg & Spinach Muffins

 Yield: 6 servings

 Time: 20 minutes

1/2 cup = 1 serving*

*always follow your surgeon's guidelines and tune into your own hunger and fullness cues.

About this recipe

These egg muffins are a winner for so many different reasons. They're soft, are high in protein and can be easily packed for meal on-the-go!

Ingredients

- 6 eggs
- 2 cups spinach, finely chopped
- Salt and pepper to taste

Directions

1. Preheat oven to 350°F (175°C).
2. Spray a 6-cup muffin pan with non-stick cooking spray.
3. In a mixing bowl, crack the eggs. Whisk well.
4. Add the spinach, salt and pepper. Stir until well combined.
5. Pour the egg-mixture into the muffin molds, until 3/4 full.
6. Place in oven and bake, about 15 minutes.

Nutrition Facts
Per Serving

68 calories
Protein 6.5 g
Carbs 15.1 g
Fiber 0.8 g
Fat 4.6 g

Recipe Notes

- Add more seasoning to the egg-mixture if tolerated well.
- Examples of herbs to add are chopped parsley, garlic powder, onion powder, Italian seasoning and rosemary powder.
- Substitute the spinach for finely chopped pre-cooked carrots for a different variety.

Carrot Overnight Oats

 Yield: 2 servings

 Prep time: 20 minutes
Soak time: at least 6 hours

 1/2 cup = 1 serving*

*always follow your surgeon's guidelines and tune into your own hunger and fullness cues.

About this recipe

This recipe is perfect if you want to prep your breakfas ahead for the next day. It only takes 10 minutes and a night in the fridge for these carrot overnight oats to become a delicious meal in the morning.

Ingredients

- 1/4 cup (40 g) carrots, peeled and grated
- 1/4 cup (25 g) rolled oats
- 8 oz (230 ml) water
- 1 cup (230 ml) skim milk
- 1/4 teaspoon cinnamon powder

Directions

1. In a small pan, add water and bring to a boil. Lowe heat and add the grated carrots. Remove after 2 minutes. Allow the carrots to cool off.
2. In another pan, add the oats and water over low-medium heat and bring to a boil, about 10 minutes
3. Remove from heat, strain and allow to cool off completely.
4. In a glass container, add the oats, milk, carrots and cinnamon powder. Mix until well combined. Add more milk if you want a smoother texture.
5. Place in fridge for at least 6 hours.

Nutrition Facts
Per Serving

94 calories
Protein 6 g
Carbs 14.4 g
Fiber 1.5 g
Fat 1.1 g

Recipe Notes

- Substitute the skim milk for almond milk or soy milk. Keep in mind that almond milk barely has any protein.
- Add softened and peeled apple or soaked raisins to create a sweeter variety of these overnight oats.

*carrot pieces for garnish, raw vegetables aren't suitable for consumption at this stage. Raisins are optional - and only when approved by your surgeon.

Baked Salmon in Foil

 Yield: 1 serving

 Time: 30 minutes

1/2 cup = 1 serving*

*always follow your
surgeon's guidelines
and tune into your own
hunger and fullness
cues.

About this recipe

Salmon is a fatty fish that provides omega-3 fatty acids
and is a great source of protein as well. Its soft texture
makes salmon a great asset to your post-op diet.

Ingredients

- 1 tablespoon olive oil
- 1 teaspoon lemon juice
- 1/2 teaspoon dill powder
- Salt and pepper to taste
- 4 oz (110 g) salmon

Directions

1. Preheat oven to 350°F (175°C).
2. In a small bowl, add the olive oil, lemon juice, dill
   powder, salt and pepper. Stir until well combined.
3. Line a baking sheet with foil
4. Place the salmon on top of the foil. Pour the olive oil
   mixture on the salmon. Make sure the salmon is
   fully coated.
5. Fold the foil around the salmon, closing the packet
   completely.
6. Place salmon in oven, bake about 20 minutes.
7. Serve immediately.

Nutrition Facts
Per Serving

288 calories
Protein 22 g
Carbs 0.2 g
Fiber 0 g
Fat 22.1 g

Recipe Notes

- You can use an air fryer instead of the oven. Make
  sure to lower the temperature to 300°F (150°C).
- Substitute the salmon for any other type of fish
  that you're cleared to have at this stage.
- Traditionally, this recipe is made with butter
  instead of olive oil. Keep in mind that butter has
  more saturated fats. Olive oil contains more
  unsaturated fats.

*lemon wedge and dill for garnish, not suitable for consumption at this stage.

Curry Lentil Soup

 Yield: 8 servings

 Time: 25 minutes

 1/2 cup = 1 serving*

*always follow your
surgeon's guidelines
and tune into your own
hunger and fullness
cues.

About this recipe

This hearty soup is perfect for a cold day. Or whenever
you crave something savory. This curry lentil soup is
100% plant-based.

Ingredients

- 15 oz (425 g) canned lentils,
  rinsed and drained
- 32 oz (950 ml) vegetable
  broth
- 1 teaspoon curry powder
- Salt and pepper to taste

Directions

1. In a soup kettle, add the canned lentils and
   vegetable broth. Slowly bring to a boil.
2. Add the curry powder, salt and pepper. Stir well.
3. Reduce heat and simmer, about 15 minutes.
4. Allow the soup to cool off.
5. In a blender (or with a hand blender), blend the
   soup until smooth.

Nutrition Facts
Per Serving

59 calories
Protein 4 g
Carbs 8.2 g
Fiber 3.1 g
Fat 0.4 g

Recipe Notes

- You can use dried lentils too. Make sure that you
  soak them overnight and increase the cooking
  time accordingly.
- If you don't have curry powder, try a combination
  of these herbs instead (if tolerated well, and
  cleared by your surgeon): turmeric powder, ginger
  powder and cumin powder.
- This recipe is also suitable for the puréed stage - if
  blended until puréed consistency.

"Chocolate" Pudding

Yield: 3 servings

Time: 5 minutes
Set time: 1 hour

1/2 cup = 1 serving*

*always follow your
surgeon's guidelines
and tune into your own
hunger and fullness
cues.

About this recipe

If you're craving chocolate, then this recipe might be
just what you need. Instead of real chocolate, we used
cocoa powder for that rich flavor. And we added
banana, avocado and Greek yogurt to get the creamy
texture that's perfect for the soft foods stage.

Ingredients

- 1 banana
- 1/2 avocado
- 1 cup (240 g) low-fat Greek yogurt
- 1/2 teaspoon cocoa powder

Directions

1. In a food processor, add the banana, avocado, Greek yogurt and cocoa powder. Blend until smooth.
2. Place in fridge to set, about 1 hour.

Nutrition Facts
Per Serving

187 calories
Protein 8.1 g
Carbs 11.7 g
Fiber 2.5 g
Fat 11.2 g

Recipe Notes

- Top with slices of banana if tolerated well and cleared by your surgeon.
- If you don't have a food processor, you can use a blender instead.

*chopped nuts for garnish, not suitable for consumption at this stage.

Meatloaf & Marinara Muffins

 Yield: 8 servings

Time: 45 minutes

1/2 cup = 1 serving*

*always follow your surgeon's guidelines and tune into your own hunger and fullness cues.

About this recipe

Meatloaf, but slightly different. These bite-sized savory muffins will keep your pouch full for long and provide you with the protein you need. If you can't tolerate bee yet, you can use ground turkey instead!

Ingredients

- 1 lb (450 g) lean ground beef
- 1 clove garlic, minced
- 1 teaspoon onion powder
- 1/2 teaspoon ginger powder
- 1 egg, beaten
- 1 tablespoon zero-sugar ketchup
- 1/2 teaspoon Worcestershire sauce
- 1/4 teaspoon oregano powder
- 1/4 teaspoon thyme powder
- Salt and pepper to taste
- 6 tablespoons marina sauce

Directions

1. Preheat oven to 350°F (175°C).
2. Spray a 12-cup muffin pan with non-stick cooking spray.
3. In a large mixing bowl, add the beef, garlic, onion powder, beaten egg, ketchup, Worcestershire sauce, oregano powder, thyme powder, salt and pepper. Mix until well blended.
4. Fill each muffin cup with the ground beef mixture.
5. Top with 1/2 tablespoon of marinara sauce each.
6. Place in oven, about 25 minutes or until well cooke inside.

Nutrition Facts
Per Serving

176 calories
Protein 18 g
Carbs 0.6 g
Fiber 0.5 g
Fat 17.1 g

Recipe Notes
- Make your own marinara sauce by blending the following ingredients: canned tomatoes, parsley, onion (powder), garlic (powder) and salt.

3-Layer Chicken "Lasagna"

 Yield: 4 servings

 Time: 45 minutes

1/2 cup = 1 serving*

*always follow your
surgeon's guidelines
and tune into your own
hunger and fullness
cues.

About this recipe

Lasagna can be a real favorite in many households around the world. But after bariatric surgery, in the soft foods stage, traditional lasagna is still a no-go. The lasagna sheets are too sticky and may cause digestive issues. But we modified this recipe so you can enjoy the taste of this Italian masterpiece too!

Ingredients

- 1 chicken breast fillet (6 ounces, 170 g)
- 1 tablespoon olive oil
- 2 eggs
- 1 1/2 cups (350 ml) marinara sauce
- 1 cup (150 g) low-fat ricotta cheese
- 1 teaspoon Italian seasoning

Toppings (optional)
- Grated Parmesan cheese
- Sliced mozzarella

Directions

1. Preheat oven to 350°F (175°C).
2. Cut the chicken breast lengthways, as thinly as possible.
3. In a skillet, heat olive oil over medium-high heat. Add the sliced chicken and bake on each side, about 7 minutes.
4. In a mixing bowl crack the eggs. Add the ricotta and the Italian herbs.. Mix until well combined.
5. Spray a baking dish with non-stick cooking spray.
6. Layer the dish with 1 layer of marinara sauce, 1 layer of egg-ricotta mixture, 1 layer of sliced chicken breast.
7. Repeat the process until all ingredients are used.
8. Place the chicken lasagna in the oven, about 20 minutes until fully cooked.

Nutrition Facts
Per Serving

269 calories
Protein 19.6 g
Carbs 7.8 g
Fiber 1.6 g
Fat 17.4 g

Recipe Notes

- Beat the chicken slices with a meat mallet to create even thinner slices of chicken breast.
- If you don't have Italian herbs, try a combination of the following herbs instead: oregano powder, thyme powder, marjoram powder, basil powder.
- Only add the Parmesan cheese and mozzarella if cleared by your surgeon and tolerated well.

Canned Crab Cakes

 Yield: 2 servings

 Time: 30 minutes

 1/2 cup = 1 serving*

*always follow your surgeon's guidelines and tune into your own hunger and fullness cues.

About this recipe

If you like crab cakes, then this recipe is for you! Canned crab is more affordable than fresh crab. A quick and easy meal to meet your protein goals better.

Ingredients

- 4 oz (110 g) canned crab meat
- 1 egg
- 1/4 cup (12 g) panko bread crumbs
- 1/4 teaspoon Dijon mustard
- Salt and pepper to taste

Dipping sauce (optional)
- Low-fat Greek yogurt

Directions

1. Preheat oven to 300°F (150°C).
2. In a food processor, add the crab meat, egg, Dijon mustard, breadcrumbs, salt and pepper. Blend until well combined.
3. Line a baking sheet with parchment paper.
4. Using your hands, make 4 small crab meat balls and flatten them. Spread them evenly on the baking sheet.
5. Place the crab cakes in the oven and bake, about 20 minutes or until golden brown.
6. Serve with Greek yogurt dip.

Nutrition Facts
Per Serving

104 calories
Protein 14 g
Carbs 4.4 g
Fiber 0.4 g
Fat 3.2 g

Recipe Notes
- You can bake the crab cakes in a skillet instead of the oven too. Use one tablespoon of olive oil over medium-high heat.
- Omit the breadcrumbs if you can't tolerated them yet. If you don't use any breadcrumbs, the crab cakes will be more difficult to knead. We don't recommend using a skillet like mentioned above, but to stick to the recipe above.
- If you don't have a food processor, use a blender instead.

Bariatric Spinach Frittata

Yield: 4 servings

Time: 30 minutes

1/2 cup = 1 serving*

*always follow your surgeon's guidelines and tune into your own hunger and fullness cues.

About this recipe

Frittata is an Italian dish with eggs, vegetables and cheese being the main ingredients. The word frittata is derived from friggere which basically means "fried". Our bariatric friendly frittata is simple: eggs & spinach - oven baked to the perfect consistency for the soft foods stage.

Ingredients

- 4 eggs
- 1 cup (230 ml) skim milk
- 1/2 teaspoon onion powder
- 1/4 teaspoon garlic powder
- 1 tablespoon olive oil
- 2 cups (80 g) spinach
- Salt and pepper to taste

Topping (optional)
- Grated Parmesan cheese

Directions

1. Preheat oven to 350°F (175°C).
2. In a mixing bowl, add the eggs, milk, onion powder, garlic powder, salt and pepper. Whisk until well combined.
3. In an oven-safe skillet heat the olive oil over medium-high heat. Add the spinach, a handful at a time, and sauté until wilted, about 2 minutes.
4. Lower heat. Spread the spinach into an even layer and pour the egg-mixture over the top. Make sure that the eggs are evenly settled over the spinach. Cook, about 2 minutes.
5. Transfer the skillet to the oven and bake until the eggs are set, about 15 minutes.

Nutrition Facts
Per Serving

114 calories
Protein 8.9 g
Carbs 3.1 g
Fiber 0.4 g
Fat 7.2 g

Recipe Notes

- Only use the Parmesan cheese as a topping if cleared by your surgeon and well tolerated.
- You can skip step 5 if you just want to make a quick egg & spinach omelet.

Blueberry Beet Smoothie

 Yield: 2 servings

 Time: 5 minutes

 1/2 cup = 1 serving*

*always follow your
surgeon's guidelines
and tune into your own
hunger and fullness
cues.

About this recipe

This nutrient-packed smoothie is perfect to satisfy a
sweet craving - while making sure you're getting your
vitamins in. The ingredients of this smoothie are low in
protein. But you can always add unflavored protein
powder to turn this smoothie into a protein shake.

Ingredients

- 1/2 cup (50 g) pre-cooked
  beet root
- 1 cup (50 g) frozen
  blueberries
- 8 oz (230 ml) water

Add-on (optional)
- Handful ice cubes

Directions

1. In a blender add the beet root, blueberries and
   water. Blend until smooth.

Nutrition Facts
Per Serving

21 calories
Protein 0.5 g
Carbs 3.9 g
Fiber 1.3 g
Fat 0.1 g

Recipe Notes

- If you can't tolerate cold drinks yet, use fresh
  blueberries instead.
- Add unflavored protein powder to your smoothie,
  to turn it into a home-made protein shake.
- Did you know that beetroot supports gut health
  after Bariatric Surgery? Also, beet root improves
  blood flow and helps to lower blood pressure.

Soft Protein Cookies

 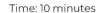

Yield: 6 servings

Time: 10 minutes

1/2 cup = 1 serving*

*always follow your
surgeon's guidelines
and tune into your own
hunger and fullness
cues.

About this recipe

Just because you had bariatric surgery, doesn't mean
that all cravings suddenly disappear. So, if you're
craving something sweet - you may want to give these
bariatric friendly cookies a try. No added sugars. No
added fats. Just basic ingredients to satisfy your sweet
tooth without compromising your protein goals.

Ingredients

- 1 medium ripe banana
- 1/2 cup (50 g) rolled oats
- 1 scoop vanilla protein
  powder
- 1 egg, beaten
- 1/4 teaspoon cinnamon
  powder
- Pinch salt

Directions

1. Preheat oven to 350°F (175°C).
2. In a food processor, add the banana, oats, vanilla
   protein powder, egg, cinnamon powder and salt.
   Blend until smooth.
3. Line a baking sheet with parchment paper.
4. Using your hands, make 6 small balls from the
   batter and flatten on the baking sheet. Spread
   evenly.
5. Place in the oven and bake, about 20 minutes,
   turning the cookies halfway.
6. Remove from oven and allow to cool off.

Nutrition Facts
Per Serving

75 calories
Protein 5.6 g
Carbs 9.4 g
Fiber 1 g
Fat 1.4 g

Recipe Notes

- Try different flavoured protein powder to switch up
  this recipe.
- Add smooth peanut butter to the batter if you're
  cleared to eat nut butters again.

QUICK
GROCERY LIST

Quick Grocery List**

Canned Goods

- Tuna
- Salmon
- Crab
- Beans
- Lentils
- Chickpeas
- Chicken broth
- Peaches*
- Pears*
- Pineapple*
- Apricots*

*in own juice or water

Frozen Foods

- Tilapia
- Tuna
- Cod
- Haddock
- Flounder
- Shellfish
- Spinach
- Green peas
- Blueberries

Dairy

- Skim milk
- Buttermilk
- Low-fat quark
- Low-fat Skyr (Icelandic dairy)
- Low-fat (Greek) yogurt
- Low-fat ricotta cheese
- Low-fat Parmesan cheese
- Eggs
- Low-fat cottage cheese

Meat, Fish, Poultry, Vegetarian

- Lean ground beef
- Lean ground turkey
- Lean ground chicken
- Chicken breast
- All white fish (eg cod)
- Shellfish (eg shrimp)
- Surimi
- Tofu
- Veal, beef and pork (loin)

Produce

- Spinach
- Carrots
- Squash
- Green beans
- Pears
- Peaches
- Pineapple
- Melon
- Apricots
- Beet root
- Bananas

Starches

- Oatmeal
- Porridge
- (sweet) Potatoes
- Quinoa
- Bulgur
- Couscous

**The items on this grocery list may not be suitable for all stages at the same time. Nor are the items exhaustive for the recipes you'll find in this book.

Quick Grocery List**

Herbs & Spices

- Onion powder
- Garlic powder
- Cinnamon powder
- Paprika powder
- Cumin powder
- Dill powder
- Parsley powder
- Curry powder
- Taco seasoning
- Italian seasoning
- Bay leaves

Other

- Zero-sugar BBQ sauce
- Marinara sauce
- Zero-sugar vanilla extract
- Cocoa powder
- Granulated sweetener (non-calorie)
- Nutritional yeast
- Dietitian approved (unflavored) protein powder and protein supplements

The items on this grocery list may not be suitable for all stages at the same time. Nor are the items exhaustive for the recipes you'll find in this book.

BARIATRIC
MEAL TIPS

5 Tips to simplify your meals after Bariatric Surgery

There are a few tips and tricks we'd like to share with you before we get to the end of this book. And here are our 5 top tips to make your eating experience after bariatric surgery easier:

1   **Use (high-protein) liquids to modify the texture of your dish**

Most dishes in the puréed and even the soft foods stage require mashing, processing or blending the food in order to get the desired texture. By adding more or fewer liquids, you can modify the texture quite easily. Here are 7 liquids you can use to make your food more moist:

- Bone broth
- Vegetable broth
- Skim milk
- Soy milk
- Buttermilk
- Low-fat Greek yogurt
- Water

2   **Add unflavored protein powder to your dish to increase the amount of protein**

The goal after bariatric surgery is to progress to a diet that consists of regular, solid foods where most, if not all protein requirements are met. But it won't be that simple right away. By adding unflavored (or flavored) protein powder to your meals, you automatically increase the amount of protein per serving.

Remember, you'll mostly rely on protein shakes to meet your protein goals in the very early stages after bariatric surgery.

3   Use different cooking styles to switch up the variety

Even though not all foods will fit right away, there are different cooking styles that you can try with the foods that you *can* tolerate right now.

Not all foods have to be cooked until all colors and flavors have faded leaving your food tasteless and unappealing. Try techniques like: steaming, grilling, sautéing, roasting, using the oven or air fryer and broiling.

As long as you follow your surgeon's guidelines and adjust the textures to your needs, there's plenty of different cooking styles to choose from.

4   Don't forget to add flavor to your food

There's a wide variety of herbs and spices to add more flavor to your food. And although you may not be able to tolerate them all, try to work with the ones that you're allowed. The herbs and spices in this book are simple, because we don't want to overcomplicate things. But there's so much to choose from. Be sure to include those different flavors to your meals to keep things interesting.

It's quite common to get bored and uninspired during the early stages eating the same foods over and over again. This is called *food fatigue*. By trying new flavors, foods and recipes - you may feel more happy, eating after bariatric surgery.

5   Protein first, produce next, complex carbs last

The priority of your meal should be protein. If you have space for your veggies or fruit, they're next. Last on your plate to eat are the complex carbs. The further you're out of surgery, the easier it tends to include a wide array of foods on your plate.

Made in the USA
Monee, IL
01 October 2022

14984717R00063